STOCK CARS

Paul Mason

W

FRANKLIN WATTS

LONDON • SYDNEY

First published in 2009
by Franklin Watts

Franklin Watts
338 Euston Road
London NW1 3BH

Franklin Watts Australia
Level 17/207 Kent Street
Sydney, NSW 2000

Planning and production by
Tall Tree Limited
Editor: Rob Colson
Designer: Jonathan Vipond

Dewey number 796.72

ISBN 978 0 7496 8696 3

Printed in China

Franklin Watts is a division of Hachette Children's
Books, an Hachette UK company.

www.hachette.co.uk

Picture credits:
BMW AG: 20, 23.
Corbis: 8 (Underwood & Underwood),
17 (George Tiedemann/GT Images).
Creative Commons: 27 (Apterygial), 29tl,
29ml (Morio), 29mr (JPMontoya.com),
29bl (Bo Nash), 29br.
Dreamstime: Cover main image (Sideline),
Cover bm, bl, br (Lawrence Weslowski Jr),
3 (Lawrence Weslowski Jr), 6 (Actionsports),
7 (Sparkyhew), 10–11 (Lawrence Weslowski Jr),
12–13 (Toddtaulman), 13 (Lawrence Weslowski
Jr), 14–15 (Walter Arce), 19 (Lawrence Weslowski
Jr), 22 (Lawrence Weslowski Jr), 24–25
(Lawrence Weslowski Jr), 29tr (Vclements).
Getty: 9t (RacingOne), 9b (Focus on Sport),
11t, 15, 16, 18 (Robert Laberge), 26–27 (Ciapix).
Istockphoto: 21 (Michael Krinke).

CONTENTS

STOCK CAR RACING

Stock car racing is filled with wheel-to-wheel racing, blink-and-you-miss-it speeds and how-do-they-do-that cornering. The amazing thing about it, though, is that the racers' cars look a bit like cars on the street!

TECHNICAL DATA

*The three closest finishes in **NASCAR** races were:*

1) 2003 Ricky Craven beat Kurt Busch by 0.002 sec.

2) 1993 Dale Earnhardt beat Ernie Irvan by 0.005 sec.

3) 2007 Jamie McMurray beat Kyle Busch (Kurt's younger brother!) by 0.005 sec.

▲ *The USA is home to many of the biggest events in stock car racing. Some races, such as the NASCAR Shelby 427 in Las Vegas, attract hundreds of thousands of spectators.*

WHAT ARE STOCK CARS?

Stock cars were originally race cars based on **stock** vehicles, which could be bought from an ordinary showroom. The race cars all had similar engines and **suspension**, so they went at similar speeds. Race finishes were often very close.

△ The tight, twisty tracks of BTCC (British Touring Car Championship) races, such as this one at Brands Hatch in the UK, are very different from the race ovals of the USA.

Today, the sport's regulations (produced by NASCAR in the USA, and the BTCC in the UK) still aim for close racing and tight finishes. Top-level stock cars usually have a 'stock' body shell, so they look like ordinary cars. Underneath this shell, however, almost every part is different from a normal car.

RACING AROUND THE WORLD

In the USA, **oval** track races are popular. These are made up of three or four bends linked by straights. The bends are sometimes **banked** to allow more speed. In Europe and Australia, **touring car** races attract big crowds. They take place on tight, twisty tracks and the cars are more closely based on stock vehicles.

BIRTH OF NASCAR

Today, the USA's NASCAR series is probably the world's top level of stock car racing. NASCAR racing is good, clean family fun. But there are those who say it has its roots in a far murkier past – the world of the moonshine runner!

MOONSHINE RUNNERS

Between 1920 and 1933, alcoholic drinks were banned by law in the USA. Criminals began moving illegal alcohol, called moonshine, around using 'moonshine runners' – the fastest drivers and cars around. Often the runners would travel in groups, and the drive turned into a race.

△ These rum runners were stranded on Daytona Beach, Florida, in December 1925 in the scramble to retrieve cases of rum floating ashore from a sunken vessel.

TECHNICAL DATA

The first NASCAR race took place on 19 June 1949 at the Charlotte Speedway. Glenn Dunnaway was the first to cross the line, but he was disqualified when he was found to have modified his car.

ORGANISED RACING

Outrunning the cops gave the drivers a taste for the thrills of racing ordinary cars. When alcohol became legal again in 1933, many drivers carried on racing just for fun. Crowds enjoyed watching the close action and stock car racing became increasingly popular.

△ *Lee Petty nicks the win at the line in the first ever Daytona 500 in 1959.*

NASCAR

In 1948, NASCAR was formed as a governing body for US stock car racing. At first, all racecars were based on showroom models. After 1973, however, teams were allowed to use specially designed parts. Meanwhile in Europe, touring cars remained based on showroom models (as they are today).

▽ *The Pontiac GTO of Richard Petty. He won the NASCAR Championship seven times in a career that ran for more than 30 years from 1960.*

ENGINES AND BRAKES

Today's top stock cars might look like souped-up versions of ordinary cars – but under the skin they are very different. A car racing in the NASCAR Sprint Cup, for example, is unlikely to have many parts that you could find in an ordinary car showroom!

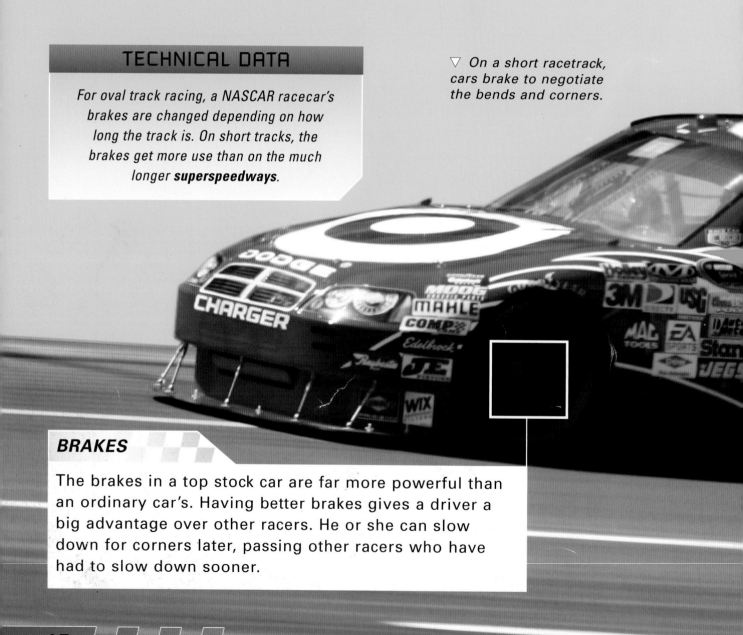

TECHNICAL DATA

For oval track racing, a NASCAR racecar's brakes are changed depending on how long the track is. On short tracks, the brakes get more use than on the much longer **superspeedways**.

▽ *On a short racetrack, cars brake to negotiate the bends and corners.*

BRAKES

The brakes in a top stock car are far more powerful than an ordinary car's. Having better brakes gives a driver a big advantage over other racers. He or she can slow down for corners later, passing other racers who have had to slow down sooner.

STOCK CAR ENGINES

Engines in modern NASCAR racecars are all the same size and use the same basic technology. Amazingly, most ordinary family cars have more advanced engine technology than a NASCAR racecar. For example, racecars use **carburettors** instead of computer-controlled fuel injection.

Touring cars are based on production vehicles that can be bought in a showroom. This means that they have access to the very latest engine technology, such as computerised tuning. But the engines in production cars are smaller than in NASCAR racecars, so they are not as powerful.

△ Mechanics set to work on the engine of a racecar during practice for the NASCAR Nextel Cup Daytona 500.

TYRES, SUSPENSION, AERODYNAMICS

Because all the cars use similar engines, stock car teams have to find other areas where they can make their car faster than everyone else's. The key changes they can make are to a car's tyres, suspension and **aerodynamics**.

Front splitter

SUSPENSION

A stock car's suspension absorbs the lumps and bumps of the racetrack, as well as the big forces of braking and cornering. The suspension is tuned to suit different racetracks. On smooth, fast tracks the suspension can be stiffer, without as much bounce.

▲ A stock car is shaped so that it can move through the air as easily as possible, as well as creating **downforce** to push it into the track and increase grip.

AERODYNAMICS

Although they are a similar shape to ordinary cars, top-level stock cars have a range of aerodynamic features:

- Splitters help control front downforce (how strongly the car's front tyres push down onto the track surface).

- Roof flaps stop the car becoming airborne at high speed.

- Rear wings provide additional downforce for more **grip**.

Roof flap

Rear wing

TYRES

Tyres make a huge difference to how much grip a stock car has. Teams choose their tyres according to the conditions and track surface (whether the track is concrete or asphalt, for example). In NASCAR, there are even different tyres depending on how steeply the circuit is banked!

TECHNICAL DATA

NASCAR teams can choose from 14 different types of tyre. On a typical race weekend, each team wears out between 9 and 14 sets of tyres! The tyres are filled with dry air or **nitrogen**.

△ This new tyre will need replacing after about 200 km. On an ordinary car, tyres will usually last at least 8,000 km!

A TYPICAL TRACK

The most famous stock car races in the USA are held on oval tracks. Oval tracks come in different lengths, but drivers always race around them in an anti-clockwise direction. There is plenty at each track for eagle-eyed race fans to see.

PIT ROAD

Each team is given a **pit stall** to perform pit stops and work on its car. The fastest qualifier gets the best stall.

GARAGE AREA

Cars are kept here when not on the track. Each team has a separate area where they can work on the car.

ROAD TRACKS

While oval tracks feature bends that only turn one way, races held on road tracks have a variety of different features. These include chicanes, long straights, hairpin bends and corners in both directions.

RACE CONTROL

Race officials use TV screens in this area to watch the race, deciding if any teams or drivers have broken the rules and what their punishment should be.

The corners on oval tracks are banked to increase the cars' speed.

TECHNICAL DATA

At many racetracks, such as the Michigan International Speedway pictured left, fans get the chance to camp on the area inside the track! This gives them a great view of the race, as well as a place to light a barbecue and socialise.

RACE STRATEGY

The fastest car doesn't always win a stock car race – often the winner is the driver whose team has worked out the best strategy, or plan, for the race. There are three key elements to team strategy: fuel, tyres and speed.

FUEL, TYRES, SPEED

Fuel and tyres are consumed quickest at top speed. Going a little slower makes them last longer. This might mean you can make fewer pit stops than your opponents.

Keeping your tyres fresh can also mean your tyres are less worn out at the end of the race and you can drive faster than the opposition. But if you go too slow earlier on, they'll be so far ahead it doesn't matter!

▽ If drivers wear out their tyres, they have to come into the pits for a fresh set. Every second counts, so teams sprint off the track once the tyre has been changed.

DRAFTING

Drafting, also known as slipstreaming, is a way of getting a bit of help from the car ahead. As it punches through the air, the car in front makes a hole in the air. A car close behind is in this hole, so it meets less air resistance than normal. Its driver can either get a little extra speed and overtake, or ease off the accelerator pedal and save fuel.

△ Every car apart from the one at the front is drafting – saving fuel and increasing their average speed.

TECHNICAL DATA

Drafting is important in long races. The cars work together to increase their average speed, taking turns at the front. But at some point, one driver leaves the group and sprints for the line – hoping that the others won't be able to catch up!

SAFETY AT THE TRACK

With speeds reaching 300 kph, safety is important in stock car racing. In the past, many spectators and drivers have been killed by crashes. Fortunately, today's cars and tracks are designed to keep the drivers and spectators safe if an accident happens.

TECHNICAL DATA

At some superspeedway racetracks in the USA, stock cars were starting to reach top speeds that were dangerous. NASCAR decided that engines had to be fitted with **restrictor plates**, limiting the top speed the cars could reach.

△ Ryan Newman crashes during the NASCAR Winston Cup Series Daytona 500. Fortunately, he was not injured.

AROUND THE TRACK

Many features make today's racetracks safer than ever before. At ovals, special barriers absorb the force of a crash and slow the car down. Touring car tracks have tyre walls that do the same job, and run-off areas that allow cars to slow down before they hit something.

Track marshals help to keep the racing safe. After an accident, they wave coloured flags to warn the drivers. If anyone drives dangerously, the race stewards can hand out a punishment.

DRIVER SAFETY

Stock cars today have many safety features that are designed to protect drivers from serious injury during an accident. In NASCAR, for example:

• A roll cage stops the driver being crushed if the car flips.

• Special tyres mean you can get back to the pits even if they have a puncture.

• Drivers wear fireproof suits, helmets and **HANS** devices.

IN THE DRIVER'S SEAT

Have you ever imagined yourself in the driving seat of a top stock car, such as a NASCAR car? You might find it a bit of a surprise – there are an awful lot more controls than in an ordinary car!

The built-up sides of the seat and headrest stop the driver being thrown sideways

Window netting keeps the driver's head and arms inside the car during an accident

TECHNICAL DATA

Stock cars are fitted with an emergency cut-off switch on the outside. This is so race marshals can switch off the car's engine and electrics in the event of a crash.

Fuel gauge   Oil pressure gauge

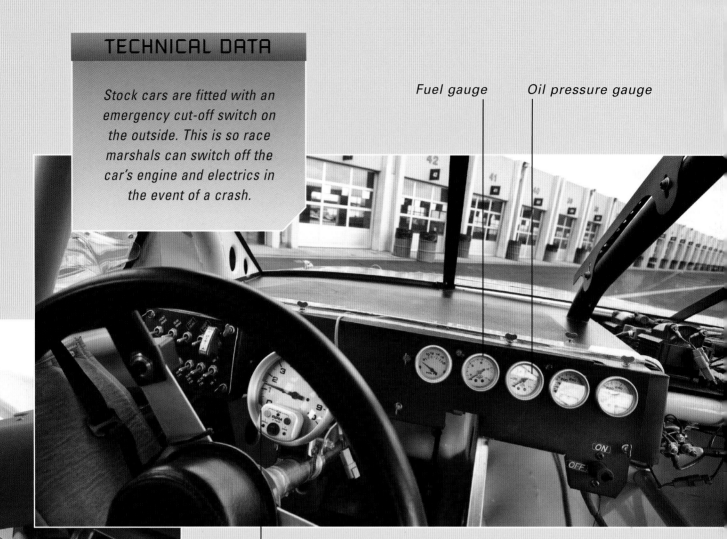

Rev counter

Removable steering wheel

Diagram of circuit

Manual (driver-operated) gearshift controls the gears

△ This is the driver's view of the cockpit. The rev counter helps the driver to know when the engine has reached maximum power, and when to change gear. Engine gauges warn the driver if something is wrong with the car.

INSIDE A STOCK CAR COCKPIT

A stock car's **cockpit** contains a huge variety of switches and controls. All through the race, the car's features help the driver squeeze as much speed as possible from it. The labels show some of the main features of the cockpit.

RACE WEEKEND

For the drivers, race weekend starts with a practice session to help them adapt the car and their driving to the track. Very quickly, however, the serious business of racing begins!

STARTING THE WEEKEND

Race weekend doesn't necessarily begin on a Saturday. Many fans arrive days before the racing starts. They camp at the track or nearby, watch the drivers practise, and hang out with the other spectators. By the time qualifying starts, everyone is very excited!

△ The start of the Bank of America 500 at the Lowe's Motor Speedway, USA. The drivers stay in qualifying order behind a pace car for several laps to allow the cars to warm up. Then the pace car moves aside, and they're off!

QUALIFYING

Qualifying decides which cars start the race at the front. The drivers aim to complete the quickest possible lap of the racetrack. The driver with the fastest lap time qualifies in **pole position**, starting ahead of the others. Second fastest starts second, and so on.

△ Spanish driver Félix Porteiro in action during practice at Estoril, Portugal, preparing for the weekend's two races in the World Touring Car Championship.

TECHNICAL DATA

Australia's Bathurst 1000 is a 1,000-kilometre touring car race. Fans know it simply as 'The Great Race'. Its greatest ever driver was Peter Brock, who won The Great Race a record nine times. In 1979, he won by an amazing six laps!

RACE DISTANCE

Stock cars race over very different distances. European touring car races can be as short as 50 km, with no pit stops. In races such as Australia's Bathurst 1,000 km and the Daytona 500 mile (805 km), the cars have to stop for new tyres and more fuel several times.

23

PIT STOPS

At a pit stop, the team can make the difference between their driver winning or losing. Each member of the pit crew has his or her own job to do, but they must all work together. A pit stop from a NASCAR race shows how teamwork is important.

TYRE CHANGE

As soon as the racecar pulls to a stop, the **pit crew** springs into action:

1. The jack man lifts the car off the ground.

2. Two tyre changers undo the wheel nuts on the right-hand side of the car, take off the old wheel and tyre, and put on a new one.

3. Two tyre carriers bring new wheels and tyres over the pit wall and hand them to the changers.

The changers move to the left-hand side of the car and start again. They signal that they are finished by stepping back and raising their hand.

Gas man with gas can

Can-catch man

1. Jack man

REFUELLING

As the tyres are being changed, a gas man fills the car's fuel tank. In NASCAR, the tank is filled from two 12-gallon (45-litre) cans of fuel. A can-catch man catches any fuel that overflows and signals when the tank is full.

Second gas can

◁ Although the drivers get most of the glory, all winning drivers need a great team behind them – especially at pit stops.

Pit crew chief

Spare tyres are handed to the pit crew over the pit wall

3. Tyre carrier

2. Tyre changer

WORLD'S GREATEST RACES

You can watch live stock car racing at tracks and circuits all round the world. There's probably one near where you live. But to see the very best racers, here are some of the places you could go.

DAYTONA 500

Run for the 50th time in 2008, the Daytona 500, in Florida, USA, is one of the biggest sports events in the world. One of its nicknames is 'The Great American Race'. The Daytona 500 is shown live around the world and is watched by over 20 million viewers.

BRICKYARD 400

Officially known as the 'Allstate 400 at the Brickyard', this is one of the biggest races of the NASCAR season. The Brickyard 400, in Indianapolis, USA, is said to attract over 250,000 spectators each year.

▷ The Brickyard 400 at the Indianapolis Motor Speedway is a highlight of the NASCAR season in the USA.

▷ Over 24 hours, the Spa-Francorchamps circuit is a test of **endurance** for the teams and their cars.

SPA 24-HOUR RACE

Running since 1929, Spa is one of the oldest touring car races in the world. The race, held at the Spa-Francorchamps circuit in Belgium, is won by the team of drivers and mechanics whose car can do the most laps in 24 hours.

TECHNICAL DATA

Juan Pablo Montoya is the only racing driver to finish in all three big races held at the Indianapolis Motor Speedway.

2000: Indy 500 (finished 1st).

2002 and 2003: Formula One US Grand Prix (4th and 6th).

2007: Brickyard 400 (2nd).

BATHURST 1000

Held on the second Sunday in October, this is probably the biggest motorsports event in Australia. Crowds of well over 100,000 people watch V8 Supercars (a kind of touring car) battle it out for over 6 hours and 1,000 km.

GLOSSARY

aerodynamic
Describing a shape around which air can flow easily.

banked
Angled. A banked turn is one where one side of the track or road is higher than the other, so the surface is at an angle instead of being flat.

carburettors
Mechanical devices for getting fuel into an engine.

cockpit
Space inside a racecar where the driver sits.

downforce
Downwards pressure, which affects the amount of grip a racecar's tyres have on the track.

endurance
Ability to do something for a long time without stopping.

grip
Stickiness or hold. If a car's tyres have good grip, it means they stick to the track well.

HANS
Short for Head And Neck Safety device.

NASCAR
Short for National Association for Stock Car Automobile Racing, the governing body for stock car racing in the USA.

nitrogen
A colourless gas that does not smell.

oval
Racetrack that is basically oval in shape. Many 'ovals' are actually more egg-shaped than oval.

pit crew
Team of people who wait in a special area (called the pits) to help the driver with maintenance and problems.

pit stall
Closed-in area in the pit lane where mechanics can work.

pole position
First place in a group of cars starting a race.

restrictor plates
Metal plates that are added to NASCAR racecars to limit their top speed.

stock
Goods that are available to buy, usually kept at the place where they are sold.

superspeedway
Oval race track at least 3 km long.

suspension
Mechanical device or devices that absorb bumps as a vehicle moves.

touring car
Racecar based on ordinary cars that are available for the general public to buy.

STAR RACERS

DALE EARNHARDT

Born: 29 April 1951
Nationality: American

One of the best NASCAR drivers ever, Earnhardt racked up seven championships and 76 NASCAR race wins. He was killed in an accident at the 2001 Daytona 500.

RICHARD PETTY

Born: 2 July 1937
Nationality: American

Sometimes known as the King of Stock Cars, Petty won 200 NASCAR races (including seven Daytona 500s) and finished in the top ten more than 700 times.

ANDY PRIAULX

Born: 8 August 1974
Nationality: Guernsey (British citizen)

Priaulx first raced karts at eight, but is best known as a touring-car driver. He is three-times World Touring Car Champion.

JUAN PABLO MONTOYA

Born: 20 September 1975
Nationality: Colombian

Montoya raced in Indy Car and Formula One before making the switch to NASCAR in 2007. He was named 'Rookie of the Year' at the end of his first season.

DARRELL WALTRIP

Born: 5 February 1947
Nationality: American

Waltrip is a three-times NASCAR champion. He won the Daytona 500 in 1989, having tried and failed 16 times before. Waltrip retired from racing in 1990.

ERIN CROCKER

Born: 23 March 1981
Nationality: American

After an outstanding junior career, Crocker made her NASCAR debut in 2005. Her career has stalled since, but she is one to watch for the future.

WEBSITES

www.nascar.com
An excellent site for anyone interested in NASCAR, with information about current results, drivers and races that are coming up. The site also has a good section called 'NASCAR 101' giving background information about stock car racing in the USA.

www.fia.com
The home page of the world governing body for motorsports, the Fédération Internationale de l'Automobile. You can keep up with the current drivers' championship, and find out where and when the races are held. This is also the place to come to find out the latest changes in the rules and regulations for all kinds of racing, including touring cars.

www.btcc.net/html/home.php
The home page of the British Touring Car Championship. It's packed with the latest news and views, lists of upcoming races and previous results, a comprehensive history of touring car racing and a chatroom to swap views and gossip on the latest events.

INDEX